My Name Means Bitter

A poetry book filled with anger, heartbreak, betrayal and injustice. There's no uplifting words to be found here, only validation that you are not alone with your pain. These poems contain the cold hard emotions and perspectives that come with navigating the bitter pitfalls of life. Healing and grieving is not a straightforward process, it's messy, confusing and unpredictable, and it takes us to depths we're at times not certain we can survive. Sometimes the only way through the pain is to express all of its unpleasantness, bitterness and resentment. Writing has always given me refuge from the dark side of life and I hope these poems will do the same for you. Wishing you the courage to survive your darkest times by whatever means necessary.

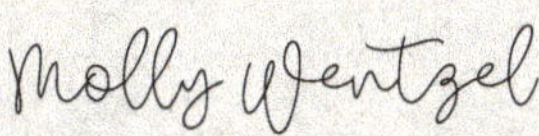

Table of Contents

Table of Contents

After the Surge

After the unstoppable wave
of rage
Depression
Hopelessness

Comes the silence
The emptiness

Each breath echoing in your eardrums
The sigh of relief felt deep
In each and every cell

In it rolls
Out it goes

The space
The peace
The in between

Something may have ended
Something might begin
After the surge

I Wish I Had Roots

Salt pours from my eyes for reasons
I don't care to remember
Loneliness suffocates me on the couch
I can escape from this life but what will it cost me?
Thankfully I find refuge outside
An observer in a world
that disregards expectations
Where my emotions can run free
without reprimand
If only I could plant my feet
in the dirt with the trees
and sway with them in the wind
I might know what home feels like

Lesson Learned

I used to believe I could bend the world to my will
Under my guidance peace would be fulfilled
Justice would be served and people would stay
But no amount of battling could keep
The greedy reaper at bay

Life humbled me thoroughly,
kept rubbing salt in my wounds
gleeful to show me just how much I could lose
I suffered in ways I didn't know existed
No escaping destruction despite my feral resistance

Now I don't fight against what needs to leave
I let it all slip through my palms as I quietly grieve
Goodbye goodbye goodbye
I whisper to all I love
It's just a matter of time before it's taken back
by abusive gods above

Duck and Weave

"You don't trust me?!
But you've known me forever!"
Exactly.
I've known you forever
I've seen you dodge & duck your responsibilities
& somehow still convince yourself that you're trustworthy
I've seen you withhold & obstruct for
your own selfish gain
Not giving a fuck who bears the pain
Of your weakness, your crimes
& your calculated moves
All while telling me
No conviction without proof
But yeah, demand I trust you
That'll sure fix it

Your aggravated sighs when I tell you I'm hurt
Your anger at me when I won't lift my skirt
Your dead eyes watching me sob again & again
Indifference the only emotion you don't have to feign

Who the fuck even are you?
& how you dare you get mad at me
After you wasted years of my life because
You're too scared to let yourself be
Whoever you really are, because I sure as hell don't know

"You don't trust me?!"
Of course not, you sociopath
And you have no one to blame
But your own weak, selfish ass

Juxtaposition

What pain it is
To be full of depth
In a mediocre world

What sadness it is
To be full of love
In a cold and hateful world

What torture it is
To get a glimpse of truth
In this illusionary world

What bullshit it is
To believe there is anything
That I can do about it

I'm More Like Ammonia

What if everything I do makes the world a little worse?
All my life I thought I could make people feel better
but here I am looking back and seeing
that everything I touch turns to dust

Stop fucking telling me I'm special when all I do is destroy
Stop fucking telling me I'm meant for big things
When all I've done is pretend I'm fine then explode
Maybe I'm not sunshine embodied
Maybe I'm more like ammonia
when it gets mixed with the wrong thing
Maybe I'm here to show people how bad it can be
They might be playing a part but hey, at least they're not me

Maybe it's time to accept that my way was the wrong one
I thought I'd teach people to avoid my mistakes
But maybe I haven't grown, I just learned to outrun them
Maybe it's time to finally admit defeat
Give myself over to the wolves and let them
Claim their victory feast

Statistics Will Never Tell the Full Story

Years have gone by and the grief still pours out of me
anytime I have a moment of stillness
I can't seem to escape the sadness
No matter how much I cry or write in my journal
It just keeps coming, layer after layer
My body didn't deserve the theft
Once by a friend, once by a stranger
I mourn what it's done to my psyche
Then I grieve for my mother, she didn't deserve it either
we deal with our pain differently
I can't stop feeling it and she can't stop denying it
I wish she'd let it flow rather than pretending it doesn't exist
then I think of all the women who've been through far worse
Or how many are being hurt at this exact moment
And I sink into an ocean of tears that just can't dry up
I feel small and hopeless over these robberies
And the injustice of being a woman in this world
To be repeatedly stolen from and having to listen to men
saying it can't be that bad and how they just don't understand
How they couldn't possibly know any predators
How they're all good to the women in their lives
How they've never seen the evidence themselves
How all of us women have to hear again and again
what upstanding gentlemen our attackers have been
How they couldn't possibly be what they're accused of being
I weep for myself
I cry for my mother
I sob for all women
who have to live in this predator's world
While no man listens, no man steps in
For all of us women with no goodness left to believe in

Unfinished

Sometimes there are no conclusions
Just endings, cold and abrupt
Sometimes the story gets cut too short
Answers not given and loose ends not tied up

Sometimes
A truth comes out
A house burns down
A loved one dies

Some stories don't conclude
They remain forever unfinished
Suspended in time and what ifs
Leaving a road perpetually untraveled
Never finding out what could have been
Those possibilities swept away by unforgiving life

I Know The Real You

One of us leaned in, tried to understand
One of us self-reflected, opened up an emotional dam
One of us kept lying, twisting, blaming
One of us continued betraying and emotionally maiming
You love a good twist, when it's on your terms anyway
You never thought I'd find the exit out of your sick game
You never thought I'd learn that you could only have me
by keeping me in confusion and insecurity
You put on a good show but have nothing to back it
Looks like someone got caught up in their own tactics
So go ahead and tell your friends how nasty I've been
They have my pity, I actually feel bad for them
That they believe they have a real friend in you
I might be the only person who holds the truth
That there's nothing behind that charismatic smile
That you'd betray them without question
in the blink of an eye
They won't learn that though because you're so calculated
you do a lil dance then stay gone so they'll never be sated
Your friends can't get close enough to see the real you
And for that, I am happy I learned to see through
I dislike knowing how many might hate me
but it's a low price I'm very thankful I'm paying

My, How I've Changed

I do not wish to grow old
I think I've seen enough
In a tale as old as time
I've lost my optimistic hope
The dishes pile up, my sweatshirt needs a wash
My credit card is maxed out and
I've been rejected by a couple thousand jobs
that I don't even want
I sleep on the couch just for the change
And check out library books just to
return them untouched

Flowers used to spring up behind me
Wherever I stepped
Now I leave a trail of dead grass in my wake
So no I don't want to grow old
I'm already the bitter crone
who hears someone's dreams
and warns them to abandon all hope

Unanswerable

If all that glitters isn't gold
And dearest friend can turn to foe
If empires rise and great women fall
How could I keep giving life my all?

Rose colored lenses slip off my nose
Acrid questions, do I dare pose?
Or is that too a gorgeous trap?
Seeking to understand or trapped like a rat?
In a never ending loop of deception
Too confused to form the questions

Is this a twisted game for bored eternals?
Or just a bad dream in someone's journal?
Are we small specks just like the Whos?
Or the aftermath of an ethereal coup?

What is left for a woman to believe in?
The answer can't lie in her god or her kin
It can only be discerned and finally found
When her mind is empty and time makes no sound

I'd Choose Different

Aware, but at what cost?
Awakened, but with such pain
Stripped of all comforts, vices, connections
The golden haze was nothing but an illusion
But looking back into it
From this cold dark awareness
It looks romantic, almost heavenly
And I can't help but wonder
Who has it better and who has it worse
People always say
"I'd do it all again, for it all made me, me"
But with that I flat out refuse to agree
If I knew all the pain that laid in wait
I'd certainly choose different
With a belief that an alternative
choice could hold peace for me
All the while knowing
that's a lie even I couldn't believe

I Should Have Run

I'd rather try too hard
than run off too soon
but dear god my love
how you delight in
playing me a fool

Unrecognized Milestones

Another hour passed
Another hour survived
I manage to comb my hair
and tell my friends I'm fine
I even get out of bed sometimes
No one understands how hard I'm fighting
Because I'm naturally pleasant and kind
but I deserve prizes for how quietly I'm battling
Do you have any idea the stamina I'm exhibiting?
Do you have any clue how close to the edge I'm teetering?
yet here I stand alchemizing the wounds,
the pain, the injustice I've been dealt
trying to leave behind a blueprint
that could save somebody else
I'm not certain anyone will ever truly understand
the depths of hell that I've lived though
and the self control I've had to command
My biggest milestone is that I've stayed alive
what's my award for my determination to survive?

The Loneliest of Lonelys

It's the loneliest of lonelys to realize you are far too much
That if you dare let out your fiercest roar
You'll open your eyes to see them cowering on the floor
And if you dare show your softness to them
Someone will take the chance to strike
Needing to destroy your depths to sleep well at night

It's the loneliest of lonelys
to realize the love you wish to express
will almost certainly never truly be met
It's the loneliest of lonelys to want so badly
to be seen and be matched
But finding that few and far between are up for the task

Don't Tell Me What To Do

Being strong is glorified but I prefer the mess
I find more honor in leaning into
the pain, the real, the truth
I find it more enlivening to howl
from the floor of my room

I won't stop sobbing until
every cell in my tired body
feels the rush of being alive again

You don't get to dictate
what I do with the pain you dealt me
I won't speed up or quiet down
I'll be rooted in place
refusing to move
until my bones feel like home again

Unfamiliar Me

I catch glimpses of what might be
Glinting off the jagged edges
Of memories and forks in the road
I used to feel trapped on my path
Now I'm paralyzed by the possibilities
That seem so real, so close
But the me I see in those potentials is unfamiliar,
too far down a road I've never taken

My fingers are bleeding from trying to put
my shattered pieces back together
Maybe instead, I'll leave them where they are
and walk to an unexpected place

And if I can walk away from those shards
That means I'm not those pieces at all
But the one who decides to leave them
That must mean that the unfamiliar me
Is somewhere within my reach
If only I have the courage to meet her

No Matter Now

The distortions became undeniably clear
I had to torch the lot, all I held dear

Insidious lies & treachery abounded
Cowardly omissions ensured
my sharp vision was clouded
The coverup far, far worse than the crime
forced me to lose all respect,
no forgive and forget this time

But no matter now
for I dream of all the people I'll meet
Like men who will worship
but still take the lead

No matter now that
I once abandoned me just to keep you
Because stronger men beg these days
for just a chance to come through

Eventually

I used to think redemption was a guarantee,
eventually

But life has taught me the only guarantee
Is time moving onward

Everything else is transient,
eventually

Only Time Will Tell

I feel bored and uninspired
Can't find a spark to save my life
I must be permanently broken
Can't save myself from strife

Is this who I really am
Without other people's problems and drama?
Empty, lifeless, a void within a body?

Is this my real state?
Or maybe just a looong, slooow emptying phase
after carrying the world's weight?

Am I inherently lost or am I right where I should be?
Healing, releasing, and unbecoming?

Only time will tell
but that thought only makes me frown
because time is like one of my old fickle friends
Unreliable and bound to let me down

Disclosure

What a crazy world we live in
To take more offense to the
Disclosure of mistreatment
Than to the assholes who continue on
doling out abuse with no remorse
Then adding mind boggling claims
of their own victimhood
What a nutty world that demands proof from victims
but hardly ever asks the accused any questions

Burnt Out

Forgive me if I move a little slow
Forgive me that I'm still entangled
in some dark scenarios
Can you not see how much I've already left behind?
Can't I get some fucking credit for changes made
while I also lost my mind?

Please I beg you, contain your scoff
I know there's more poison I need to cast off
But my body needs time, which I've already mentioned
To adjust to this new unfamiliar dimension
I've changed my friends and location
Distanced from family and got a new vocation
But you seem to have this fixation
of telling me to leave with obvious impatience

So yes I'm moving slow but
I'm burnt out on change
I'm not ready to lose the love
I thought was for the ages

Love From Afar

I think of my mom as a child and
wish I was there to take her away
There are so many people I will never forgive
for the way they treated her
She deserves fun
She deserves people who treat her well and lift her up
She deserves to be hugged
and told none of it was her fault
She deserves so many apologies from this selfish world
I became a fighter on her behalf
I am who I am because
I wanted to heal my mother's wounds
I hate that nothing I did could show her
how deserving she is of healing and tenderness
I wish she knew I pushed so hard
because she deserves everything she's ever wanted,
because I wanted to bring her the joy she deserves
I wish I could make her know what I know
I wish I could save her from the pain our family passes
down to each other
I tried so hard and nothing worked
so I had to settle for saving myself
hoping she'll eventually find her way to me
I hope she knows it's never too late
to have the life she deserves,
That the rules are all made up and people will talk anyway
so she might as well shock them all
and make them eat their words
I hope one day we can be together again
I hope she knows how deep my love runs
even though it now has to come from afar

In The Depths of Despair

Help me
Help me
Someone help me

Back up
Back up
Leave me be

Help me
Help me
Someone help me

Jumping Through Hoops

I raged with anger, you said
Stop, you're scaring me

So I cried and cried, you said
Stop, I hate being reminded of your pain

So I shared my needs and feelings, you said
Stop, why are you so damn hard to please

So I fell silent and apathetic, you said
Gosh, you make me so happy

You didn't think I'd ever notice
that being a quiet doll by your side
was the only time you ever "loved" me

Elemental

The elements don't demand I fall in line
The breeze flows as it will
And caresses me as I do the same
The trees sway,
keeping their own time while I dance off beat
and they still love me without shame
Water always finds a path of ease
Yet doesn't scold me for my difficulties
And fire, formidable fire, invites me
To be blinding and ferocious
Never once trying to dampen my blaze
I am accepted just as I am in the shade of the trees
It's live and let live here unlike the Land of the Free

I Keep My Distance Now

I died on the hill of optimism
Crucified by my own daft heart
That could only see the good in others
Love could not possibly be real
I've lived many lives in these 32 years
And all I've witnessed is greed
and playing hot potato with responsibility
I'm not sure I've ever known real love
From lover friend or clan
I tell myself it exists because it lives in me
But we probably all tell ourselves such
Comforting falsehoods to survive another day

Nowhere to Turn

I can't do this anymore
I am overwhelmed at the pain in the world
How can I keep on living
when there's so much suffering I can't change
No money to buy a distracting treat
No weed to lift me into action
No hope to fool myself into better days ahead
All I can do is write these pointless poems and cry
stupid privileged white woman tears
I feel guilty for having my own pain while
The half the planet is being bombed and brutalized
I feel powerless, small and useless
I feel like I'm complicit in all of the evil in the world
The old me would have been in the streets yelling at cops
Organizing food drives and imploring people to care
but I'm struggling to just make it through the day
No job, no available credit, no trust in my heart
The gas in my car has to be rationed,
my power might get turned off
From morning til night my mind tells me I'm a failure
The only thread keeping me here is my cat
she's the last thing I have to hold onto
I watch as she grows older
And as her minutes tick away, so do mine
I beg god to tell me how to keep her healthy and alive
And part of me knows I'm begging for me too
Because if she goes I go
I'm scared for that day to come
So I ruin all the days leading up to it
with my never ending dread
I don't want to be alive anymore
I wonder if Sugar feels that way too
And if it's my fault, if I'm a burden on her
I've ruined a lot of good things in my time
But Sugar's life is the worst one

Am I Safe Now?

When I'm drawn to someone new
I find myself wondering how long it will be
Until I'm pulling their poisoned tipped
"I love you"s
from between my shoulder blades
Leaving an open wound where
Their loving hands should lay
I desperately hope my karma
has finally been paid
I long to be held, finally,
in a soft and loving way

i'm too tired

who will save me from myself?
i seem to love to lay on the tracks
and to jump in front of bullets
love only comes from tragedy
so i offer myself up as sacrifice

now my soul is far too tired
to armor up and
find yet another dragon to slay
to follow siren calls toward another
inevitably ungrateful heart
that will likely only tear my soul to pieces

so who will be the hero now?
who will take the bullets in my absence?
i'm too tired to care

Irreconcilable Differences

Despite all the pain you gave me
I have nothing but hope for you

Despite all the chances I gave you
You having nothing but blame for me

My Pain Serves Me Well

Forgive myself? Absolutely fucking not
I let myself be abused and betrayed
In case you somehow forgot

I refuse to forget the malicious ways
I let myself be treated
So I don't let down my guard
and allow the past to be repeated

I cling tightly to my pain knowing full well
the worst traitor in my midst is my very own brain
If I don't keep my feet to the fire
then I might just find myself back in cross-wires
of my very own making because I can't seem to see
Who is a friend and who wants to hurt me

To forgive myself is just not the move
I'll punish myself forever
to protect me from the likes of you

Somewhere Else

I can't make sense of up or down,
if I'm past or present here or now
I spend my days trying to anchor
So I don't get swept away with the doubt
At times I'm joyful at the beauty of life
And others I feel nothing but
Thick darkness blocking the light
I'm so tired of fighting
and it's never worked before
So I wait for sweet death and relax into the void
I wait for some god figure to save me
Or maybe just a new dimension to appear
another world where people see the value in me
And don't need to destroy and lose me
Before they realize what they've done

Acceptance

A villain doesn't live here anymore
You believe that you gave me your all
And while I know that's not true
Truth bears no weight compared to belief
In your world, anyway

I won't be mad at you anymore
Most of the time, anyway

I should have realized as
I gave you more time
You were lying to your own face too
Never just mine

The End

I wanted us to overcome
I wanted us to rise above
But now I'm standing alone
at the end of the world
My soul is relieved to be on its own
but my heart will never understand
Why you couldn't be honest
Why you couldn't grow
Why you'd rather push me away
than face the uncomfortable together
Why you'd rather make me an enemy
than just fix what you broke
We could have had it all
It was written in the stars
I had to let go of our possibilities
and accept who you really are

Why I stay

I'm breathing you in
Plucking your essence from
The sweet rare moments
that arise every few weeks
It's never fulfilling, never enough
It's only a ghost of you sitting with me
And I know that I should go
because we are long gone
But I tell myself
please, not yet
Just one more lie
Just one more breath

My Name Means Bitter

Hope seems to be a tool of the darkness
Trust is just a game of the manipulative
THIS is the bad place
I wonder how many demons laugh together
About how easy it is to get me to hope and trust
Even in the most hopeless conditions
When I'd rage against the world growing up
My mom would tease me with the reminder
that my name means bitter
Look ma, there's no sunshine left in me
Are you proud?
You're finally right

Worship

Half-loved my whole life
Lazy lovers left me unsatisfied
I've suffered enough theft to say
Only worship will have me look your way
Now men must prove they know I'm divine
Only then will the gates open and
Oh how blessed they'll be
to be mine

Is He Out There Somewhere?

Our love is dead and gone
and I certainly don't want it back
But as the dust settled
I couldn't help but wonder what if
If only you hadn't lied and if only T hadn't died
If only you knew I wasn't an enemy
But your most adoring advocate

Did you ever love me or was that a lie too?
Was it all an act to protect you from your wounds?
You played the doting partner so well
I'll never know what was real and what was contrived
that shit still keeps me up at night
Did you laugh to yourself sometimes
About how easily I fell for your omissions?
Did all your boys help you hide indiscretions,
Then give me a big hug at our next family dinner?
Did that man I love exist anywhere at all?

Is there a wormhole somewhere
that would lead me back to the real you?
The one you pretended to be?
I'd cross space and time to find that man that I adored
Our names would echo around galaxies and
planets unknown would know of my quest
I'd dedicate my life to getting back to him
I'd never stop searching, never give up on us
If I knew that man really existed somewhere, anywhere
If only he was real

What a shame he never existed at all
But hey on the bright side
Now I don't have to spend my life
traversing the stars

Anything Can Be Poetry

Thank god
anything can be poetry
because all I have to say
is fuck this backwards world
that brutalizes and traumatizes
then demands business as usual
If you don't comply, doesn't matter
you'll eventually be forced back in line

Since art can be anything
and the world has no rules
Note down that this bitter writer
is cursing out the heavens
for being so cruel

Language Barrier

We spoke different languages

He couldn't comprehend that I don't bluff
I mean what I say

I couldn't comprehend that he lied
His words were only to make me stay

I Hate a Man in Uniform

Where do you turn when predators wear uniforms?
Who do you turn to when they are the law?
How do you stomach the parades and applause?
How does one feel safe when we know the dark truth?
That weak men love uniforms as a way to hide proof
Their buddies all vouch for their goodness and valor
While women and children's innocence are being devoured
By their crimes, their entitlement and disgusting behavior
But sure, let's stand and salute our predatory saviors
Who talk a big talk about protecting communities
From bad guys that don't exist across seas and inner cities
Who will protect us from monsters who are real threats?
The weak men who abuse power so they can try to forget
Their own emptiness, insignificance, how they've been rejected
Making arrests for overtime to buy their dream houses
Using databases to search histories of friends & potential spouses
Violating privacy and destroying lives for personal gain
I'm so tired of public servants believing they are ordained
How does one trust in the law of the land
When we know uniforms give unfit men an upper hand
That they could never achieve without help from their cosplay
Are you great men if you can't admit some in your ranks
are guilty of foul play?
For fear accountability will erode your own benefits
you willfully ignore rapists and white supremacists
For that lack of integrity, I'll always spit in your direction
Uniforms hear this rhetoric and say "don't call me for protection!"
Angry they're not receiving the expected genuflection
Sweetie you're not a god and you're not owed any respect
If you refuse to do the job, to serve and protect

You're a Fucking Coward

She didn't deserve any of it
And you're a coward about it all?
She's out here embarrassed she loved you so hard
and you're still the reason she has to stay on guard
She wanted to forgive
But you wouldn't fucking stop
Now you're the dead weight
She's grateful she dropped

Too Far Gone

What happened to my brain?
It used to be filled with facts, stories,
fun information and exciting ideas
Ways to help people and
make everything better
Now there's only rage, fog and
bad memories
I assumed I'd bounce back
Like I did each time before
But maybe that last blow
Finally did me in

Vigilante Samaritan

I will never leave someone unprotected
Whether loved one, stranger, even worst enemy
If I see injustice or undeserved violence
No matter how big or how small
I refuse to let it go on without intervention
I know what it's like to be
Left to fend for myself
The deafening silence
and the reddening of my cheeks
When no one steps in
Left to carry the shame because
if no one defended me, I must be undeserving
Surrounded by rabid beasts yet those with weapons
Sit back and say "it's not my fight"
I can count on a few fingers how many times in my life
someone stood up for me
but if I had to count my scars from friendly knives
it would take me all night

The Weight of a Thousand Women

I feel the weight of a thousand women
Heavy on my heart
I lit the match and blessed the blaze
As it heralded a new start
For me, for them, for all who came before
Next I rested, soft and slow
Endless tears coursing down in flow
I loved each drop for the price it had paid
To glide down my skin
In their bitter cascade
Then I let myself be seen in all my glory
Joy and fear tugged at my heart but
I embraced every tremor knowing
Many women would say the same thing
If only they had my luxurious safety
Sometimes I pretend I have no responsibility
No need to write or speak or sing
Until they come from the past to
visit me once more and again
I feel the weight of a thousand women
Heavy on my shoulders
Silenced, robbed, forced into submission
They remind me that fate has lined up
To place me in the most perfect position
To share our collective pain so they may finally rest
Satisfied only when they've been heard
At peace only when it's all been expressed
I so badly want to be a no-named being
living freely on the wind
But I have the weight of a thousand women
Heavy on my soul
and they demand I collect payment
from those who have maliciously played their role

You Can't Tell the Difference

What a strange feeling to know
I am leaving and that
You can't tell the difference
Just another way I know you don't love me
I'm just a body to stave off your fears
You don't care how much you destroy me
Or how miserable you are within your act
As long as I stay and keep you company
As long as you have someone to use as a shield

Affirmations

I'm not overreacting
I'm not mean
I'm not crazy

You lied, a lot
You continued to be outed
never confessing yourself
You told me you were totally see through
But of course that was another lie
It always got turned back on me
like my questions were the problem

I'm not crazy
I'm not mean
I'm not overreacting

Differing Opinions

Are you a good man
Or are you just quiet?
Are you a good man
Or do you just sidestep the fight?
Are you a good man
Or do you just straddle all the sides?
Are you a good man
Or are you just good at deflection?
Are you a good man
Or do you just leave out the parts that show
You are most definitely not?
I may be loud but
at least people know who I really am
I may be aggressive but
at least I have a spine
I may be flawed but
at least I can look at my reflection
Are you a good man?
How predictable that you think so

Try Me

I can't believe how long I spent
Apologizing to you for how your abuse hurt me
How your deflections and circular words worked
And had me believing I was the one causing pain
Now that I cut loose from your cinderblocks
That kept me drowning in your murky waters
You think you get to continue on telling your lies
About how I just wouldn't let it go and how
My rage scared and confused you
You think you get to say look how crazy she is
Writing whole books when
no one else would even be upset
If I were you
I'd sit down and shut the fuck up
because one of us is
a coward a fraud and a schmooze
And one of us
has a truth coated chip on her shoulder
and nothing left to lose

Be the Balance

Oh Aurora
What do you mean to me?
The light after the dark
The coming of the day
You seem so sweet and warm
A hazy glow lighting the way
But I can't overlook
The turbulence you bring
The break of dawn
The expulsion of darkness
You are the ending and the beginning
Oh Aurora
You are everything to me

Small Moments

What do I do in my darkest of times?
How is it that I keep going?

For me, it's hardly ever profound
Not some big philosophical moment
Where I ponder the ripples of ending it all
and change my mind
Sometimes it's simply just coffee

Telling myself that thirty more minutes of living won't hurt
So let's make one more pot and savor
One of my favorite things
hazelnut coffee with the perfect amount of cream
And that leads to a refill taken out to the deck
A neighbor waves and I force a smile
And I'd think maybe it could wait til tomorrow

Sometimes it's Sugar trotting into my room
The sweet sound of her collar overlaid with impatient meows
Since I haven't played her favorite game yet today
So I chase her around and she pretends to run away
We end up watching birds together in a sunny window
And I'd think I'd be happy forever if these moments continued

Sometimes a friend sends me a ten minute voice memo
With every detail of a funny interaction
I laugh at their stories and have questions that need answers
Friends don't know they're saviors with their simple distractions
I tell myself I can be okay because I have someone like that

So how do I keep going in the darkest of times?
It sort of just happens, kind of like life

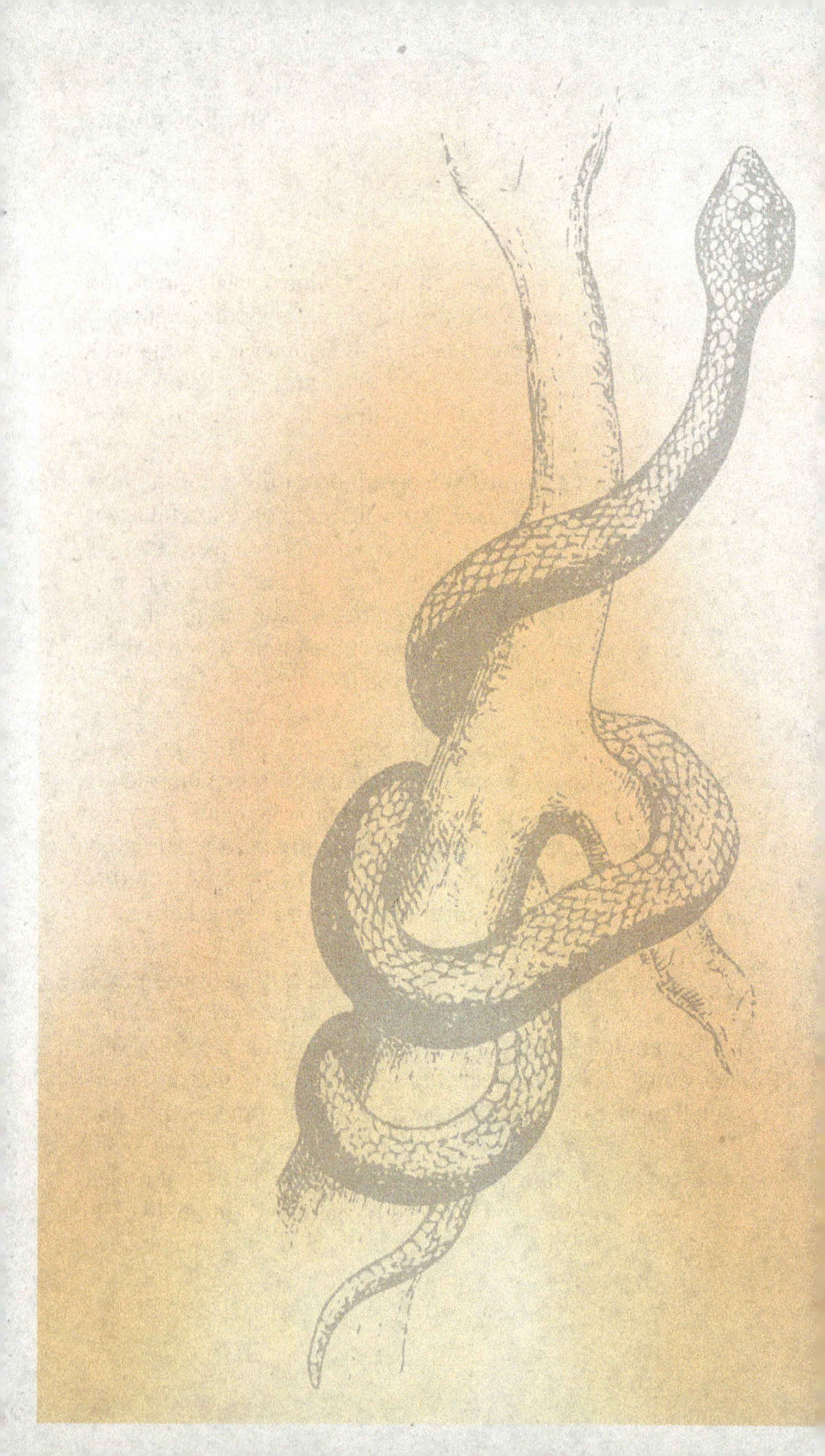

Reclamation

I want to feel safe to finally unleash and express
But the risk is too much for me I have to confess
So I take the easy way out and once again stay quiet
Although every cell within me knows I'm here to start riots
I'm meant to help other people get angry
To break from their lying partners and dysfunctional families
I know I'm a catalyst that's meant for good trouble
But I'm still having flashbacks to being trapped in the rubble
Those days are long gone but I fear they never really end
So I keep it all to myself because I'm still on the mend

I wish I could say I moved on with ease
And am ashamed to admit there's still a quake in my knees
And a catch in my throat, which only enrages me
How dare they hop on like greedy little fleas
and steal not only my love, trust and empathy
But now also my present, my expression, my bravery
How dare they cast me the villain and move on with their lives
As I pick up my pieces they slashed with rusted knives
My words long to be heard but my body remembers
How love can turn callous and friends line up to dismember

Yet no matter how deep my desire for safety
There's a pull in me to share it all anyway
To pass my flame on to some other lost person
To forge a path forward despite my fearful aversions
So I write and record despite how terribly I shake
I ignore the whispers and wave hello to the snakes
I look around at the cold ashes and realize it's time
Time to stand tall and reclaim the power that's mine
Time to speak up and share unfortunate truths
Time to make enemies quake in their boots
Time to recoup, rebuild and receive
Time to show everyone what I'm here to achieve

GGR

Join the Revolt at

www.thegoodgirlrevolt.com